THE
DIVERSITY POCKE

WITHDRAWN

by Linbert Spencer

Drawings by Phil Hailstone

"I would recommend the pocketbook to managers who want to understand the whole range of issues around what is meant by diversity and what is best practice. It is clear, brief, mercifully free of jargon and helps the manager take practical steps to implement best practice in their own organisation."
Barbara M Stephens OBE

"A great overview, packed with ideas and practical suggestions. At its heart is the idea that everyone is unique and should be treated as such - something that 99 out of 100 organisations need to do more of. Highly recommended."
Andrew Strivens, Chief Operating Officer, Weil Gotsh

Published by:
Management Pocketbooks Ltd
Laurel House, Station Approach,
Alresford, Hants SO24 9JH, U.K.
Tel: +44 (0)1962 735573
Fax: +44 (0)1962 733637
E-mail: sales@pocketbook.co.uk
Website: www.pocketbook.co.uk

This edition published 2004.
Reprinted 2005, 2007.

© Linbert Spencer 2004.

British Library Cataloguing-in-Publication
Data – A catalogue record for this book is
available from the British Library.

ISBN 978 1 903776 03 2

Design, typesetting and
graphics by **efex ltd**.   Printed in U.K.

CONTENTS

CONTENTS

1NTRODUCTION

WHO SHOULD READ THIS BOOK?

This book is for everyone with responsibility for directing, managing, supporting or influencing team members or other work colleagues.

For directors, executives and senior managers it offers specific advice and guidance on how to provide more effective leadership in terms of diversity and equality.

Middle managers will discover what's in it for them if they get good at managing the inclusion of all their people all of the time and utilize their diverse experiences effectively.

First line managers and supervisors will be introduced to ways in which they can inspire all their people and create value from the diversity of their teams.

WHY DIVERSITY MATTERS

Actively valuing diversity and managing inclusion enables organisations to consistently deliver more to more of their customers/clients more of the time, by helping more of their people to be more engaged with their work more of the time.

Diversity matters because:

- A diversity of perception, thinking and approaches - all aspects of which are more likely when a group is made up of people from different backgrounds - adds value to organisations

- It is morally right, socially desirable and economically sensible to combat discrimination, promote equal opportunity and value difference

- By increasing the involvement of employees, whose whole-hearted contribution organisations have previously failed to harness, the quality and quantity of their output will be increased

THE FOUR A's

When it comes to deliberately seeking to be more profitable and/or more effective at reaching different clients or customers, understanding the implications of diversity matters a great deal. Remember the four A's in the context of achieving greater effectiveness and profitability:

1. **Access to markets or clients is vital** for the survival and growth of any enterprise. If an organisation does not understand the nature of a particular marketplace and/or client group then getting access will be difficult, if not impossible. Organisations that fail to reflect the diversity of the marketplace and/or client group risk being shunned by those markets or clients in the long-run.

2. **Attractiveness to employees and investors is key**. Truly successful organisations are attractive places to those who would invest their time and energy and to those who would invest their money, or their clients' money. Valuing diversity and effective equal opportunity practice are just as important as corporate ethics, being a good employer and providing training when it comes to attracting investors.

    In the continuing struggle to find talented employees, diversity is an attractive draw. All of us would prefer to work in an environment where our unique contribution is sought after and valued. Also, talent doesn't come in one size, colour, gender, sexual orientation or from the same academic background.

THE FOUR A's

3. **A**nomie in society: Anomie defines the state where there is total lack of social or moral standards when individuals or groups are alienated from the wider society. If particular groups conclude that they have no stake in society they are likely to believe that no matter what they do, however antisocial or unacceptable, it won't matter because they have nothing to lose.

    Maintenance of a stable society is clearly desirable and the implications for the economic and social well-being of the nation are self-evident. Ensuring that no section of our society is in a state of anomie is not only the responsibility of the 'social agencies', it is just as much a bottom-line business concern as making sure head office overheads are kept in check.

    No corporate entity, whether private or a public service provider, has the luxury of disowning society. Properly functioning, vibrant communities are crucial for our continued economic health and well-being.

THE FOUR A's

4. **Avoiding the cost of discrimination.** If ever there was an unnecessary and damaging cost to an organisation, then the cost of discrimination is it. When organisations discriminate, the cost comes in a package. The package contains bad publicity, damage to staff morale, increased absenteeism and staff turnover, and of course a financial penalty.

   For organisations that discriminate, paying the price can persist long after the offence. Loss of reputation in particular can dull organisational effectiveness and profitability for many years.

Better access to markets and clients, attractiveness to potential employees and investors, pre-empting anomie in society and avoiding the cost of discrimination are some of the reasons why diversity matters.

DIVERSITY AND EQUAL OPPORTUNITY OVERVIEW

EQUAL OPPORTUNITY

Equal opportunity and diversity are not the same things. Many people use the terms as though they were interchangeable. They think that 'diversity is what we call it now'. This is a serious error with important implications for the decisions an organisation might take in addressing diversity and equality issues.

Equal opportunity is about:

- Tackling irrelevant discrimination and dealing with inequality

- Fairness, decency, respect and high standards of behaviour between individuals and groups

- Demonstrating the will to extend yourself for the purpose of nurturing the growth and development of others

EQUAL OPPORTUNITY

In corporate terms, equal opportunity is a concept underpinned by legislation. It requires organisations to provide relevant and appropriate access for the participation, development and advancement of all individuals and groups. In turn, equal opportunity requires individuals and groups to conduct themselves in particular ways when interacting with others.

From an individual perspective, experiencing equal opportunity is believing that you have access to, and real choice to participate in and/or contribute to, activities or processes, and that you are receiving relevant and appropriate treatment in relation to your ability and circumstances.

DIVERSITY AND EQUAL OPPORTUNITY OVERVIEW

DIVERSITY

Diversity is a given. It is not an option or something to decide to have or not to have. Where there are two or more people, you have diversity. Diversity is difference and we are all different from each other.

Our differences include:

- Family background
- Age
- Ethnic origin
- Gender
- Physical abilities, qualities and appearance
- Nationality
- Sexual orientation

- Educational background
- Marital status
- Parental status
- Religious beliefs
- Life and work experience
- All the other experiences that have touched our lives or influenced our thinking

DIVERSITY

Differences between us give us a unique range of attributes and characteristics and a distinctive view of the world. Customers and clients are diversity personified.

Organisations wanting to be more successful therefore need to recognise, capitalise on and maximise the diversity of their staff. The starting point for organisations is to recognise the value of, and then actively seek to benefit from, the diversity of their staff team.

DIVERSITY

Our staff teams have additional layers of diversity that we need to take account of. As well as exhibiting most if not all of the differences listed earlier, they may also be:

- Part-timers
- Work-share partners
- Temporary staff
- Home workers
- Telecommuters

- Sub-contractors
- Consultants
- Support staff
- Specialists
- Remote workers

We need to recognise and actively seek the benefits afforded by these differences.

SIMILARITY

There is a natural tendency for humans to gravitate towards people they perceive as similar. We feel comfortable, at ease, secure and able to be ourselves when we are with people like ourselves. Similarity then is generally the order of the day. The old saying 'birds of a feather flock together' resonates strongly in most social settings and in many organisations.

Although most organisations say that they want individuals to bring different and innovative approaches, in practice, their behaviours often suggest that difference is of little or no value and similarity is of great importance. This is usually not conscious or deliberate. But unless deliberate and positive action is taken to recognise, acknowledge and promote the value of diversity, then the old order will prevail.

It is important to note here that this can be - and often is the case - without there being any breach of equal opportunity legislation or organisational policy.

DIFFERENCE ADDS VALUE

Uniformity holds organisations together, but there needs to be sufficient diversity to stop them from dying. For any system to survive there needs to be sufficient difference within it to cope with environmental change amongst many other things. Difference adds value.

Our similarities hold us together and help us to work together. Our differences not only keep the organisation alive and resilient, but also make our work more effective and efficient.

Similarity and diversity are like two sides of the same coin. Both sides are necessary if the coin is to be of value. The more tightly similarity and diversity are bound together, the greater the value of the 'currency'. Pulling them apart simply devalues the currency.

Organisations need to help their people to understand and value those things that they hold in common and which bind them together. At the same time, they need to recognise, acknowledge and capitalise on the differences their people bring into the workplace, and consistently encourage them to display and utilize those differences.

DIVERSITY AND EQUAL OPPORTUNITY

To benefit from diversity organisations must have a clearly stated and robust equal opportunities policy. *Benefiting from diversity is the 'end' and equal opportunity policies and processes are part of the 'means'.*

Individuals who are members of, or associated with, traditionally marginalised groups (minority ethnic communities, disabled people, gay men and lesbian women, women in certain roles and so on) need the support and protection of equal opportunity policies to ensure that they have redress should they suffer discrimination.

Effective equal opportunity practices must be in place if organisations are to benefit from diversity. However, it is possible to have effective equal opportunity policies, processes and practices in place and not reap the benefit of diversity.

One of the reasons for this is that in addressing equal opportunity issues, it is necessary to focus on those groups and individuals who have been and are most disadvantaged. Focusing on disadvantage is clearly important, but in practice this almost always results in policies, processes and activities designed to prevent or respond to discrimination and little else. *Releasing the energy that human diversity potentially brings into an organisation requires far more than an anti-discrimination focus.*

(19)

DIVERSITY AND EQUAL OPPORTUNITY

Equal opportunity rules and policies must be adhered to even when attempting to create greater diversity in particular departments or units or at particular levels in the organisation.

Organisations may face conflicting priorities from time-to-time whilst pursuing an equal opportunity and diversity agenda. 'Should we promote a really good minority ethnic or female candidate who has the right competencies and experience, or should we have an open competition and risk them not getting through?'

It is of paramount importance that, at times like these, an organisation is clear about its values, vision and priorities. They can act like a homing device to guide the debate and provide all stakeholders with a basis for addressing the issue, and a powerful means of reaching a conclusion that makes sense to all concerned, even if there is not unanimous agreement.

DIVERSITY AND EQUAL OPPORTUNITY

Frederick Herzberg, the renowned American psychologist said: 'Man has two sets of needs. His need as a human to grow psychologically and his need as an animal to avoid pain'. In the work context, he named two factors to meet the needs - motivation and hygiene.

Valuing diversity and equal opportunity can be seen as addressing both sets of needs. Viewed in this way we can perhaps understand why 'not being discriminated against' does not of itself inspire people. Effective organisations need to pay equal attention to both motivation and hygiene factors.

Motivation factors enable satisfaction through:
- Responsibility
- Personal development
- Recognition
- Achievements
- Influence
- **Valuing diversity**

Hygiene factors stop dissatisfaction through:
- Job security
- Salary
- Working conditions
- **Equal opportunity**

(21)

MANAGING INCLUSION

It has become fashionable to talk about managing diversity. I fully understand why and how this has come about. Indeed, in many ways I have to share some responsibility for the phrase being in common use in equal opportunity and diversity circles. In April 1991 I organised what I believe was the first 'managing diversity' conference for executives and senior managers in the UK. Even with hindsight, I still think it was an appropriate focus at the time. However, more than a decade on my thinking has developed.

For many people, the term 'managing diversity' usually conjures up an image of difficulties and problems that must be dealt with. Consequently, courses, programmes and policies called 'managing diversity' are often perceived - and frequently subconsciously received by the participants - as addressing the 'problems' of diversity rather than the opportunities it offers. This is not helpful, to say the least.

MANAGING INCLUSION

Managing diversity is impossible.
Diversity is like time in this
respect. We have it whether we
like it or not. We can use it
well, or abuse it, make the
most of it or waste it, but
what we cannot do is
manage it.

When it comes to using
our time more productively what we
try to do is to manage ourselves better.

When our focus is diversity, the
intention is to increase the benefits we
derive from diversity. To do that, we
have to **manage inclusively.**

MANAGING INCLUSION

ASSUMPTIONS

There are several simple assumptions on which the need to 'manage inclusively' and its centrality in terms of diversity are based:

1. Most teams or work groups have members who are not fully engaged in the work of the team and, as a consequence, the team operates at less than 100%, sometimes a lot less than 100%

2. Often, team members who are not fully engaged in the work do not feel included in the team

3. The individuals who feel excluded often include a disproportionately high percentage of members of 'traditionally marginalised' groups

4. There are large numbers of people in organisations who do not feel they are included in, and therefore do not fully contribute to, the work of their teams

MANAGING INCLUSION
EXCLUSION COMES AT A PRICE

In a recent survey, the Linbert Spencer Consultancy asked thousands of managers what proportion of their people they believed were not contributing fully to their teams. Their answers ranged from 30% to 50%. The cost to organisations in terms of productivity and creativity must be enormous.

Organisations who want to maximise the quality, productivity and sustainability of their products and services need to strive to engage fully the commitment, abilities, energy and diversity of perceptions, beliefs and approaches of all their people all of the time.

To achieve this, organisations need to understand the critical importance of managing inclusion, and seek to develop the skills of their people to be competent managers of inclusion.

DIVERSITY AND EQUAL OPPORTUNITY OVERVIEW

MANAGING INCLUSION

STEREOTYPING, PREJUDICE AND DISCRIMINATION

Stereotyping happens all the time everywhere. Our failure to recognise when we are stereotyping and our lack of awareness of the implications are the issues. Every time we think we know all about someone, because we've worked with lots of people 'like them' before, we fool ourselves.

Whenever we catch ourselves stereotyping - but think it's all right because it's a 'positive stereotype' - we delude ourselves. Positive stereotypes unwittingly set certain standards for the individuals concerned. If these people fail to live up to the standards, even though they may have 'delivered' no less than those who did not fit the particular stereotype, then we will say they have failed.

Stereotyping leads us to pre-judge individuals and pre-judgement may cause us to discriminate in relation to them. Understanding our own proneness to stereotype is vital if we are to get good at managing the inclusion of others.

If you think you never stereotype, consider asking someone you spend time with for some feedback.

MANAGING INCLUSION

WATCH OUT FOR THE DRIPS

It will be obvious to all of us that when people receive negative treatment of physical or verbal abuse, because of their gender, ethnic origin, disability, nationality or whatever, they will feel excluded and subsequently function less well.

Negative treatment comes in a variety of forms and frequently the 'victims' don't even feel able to complain. They may be ignored, not asked if they want something from the shop when someone goes for sandwiches, or never asked about their time off or holiday. They may belong to a group about which there are frequent jokes and/or unflattering comments, though they will be assured that they are not included in the comments. I think of these things as low-level negative treatment.

Low-level negative treatment can be likened to the drip from a leaking gutter when it rains. The manager or supervisor isn't always around 'when it's raining', so doesn't notice. If they do notice, they don't think a little drip will be a problem. However, dripping water from the guttering will, over time, erode the concrete path below. In the same way low-level negative treatment will eventually destroy people's effectiveness. Managers and supervisors need to watch out for the drips and ensure that they are addressed promptly before erosion sets in.

DIVERSITY AND EQUAL OPPORTUNITY OVERVIEW

MANAGING INCLUSION

TREAT PEOPLE WELL

Become expert at actively and deliberately treating people well. Make sure all your people know and understand the quality standard required of them, that you believe in them and that you will provide the necessary help they need to reach and maintain the standard.

- Invest time in getting to know all your people - their areas of experience, knowledge and skills

- Deliberately find ways of using the experience, knowledge or skills that people bring

- Praise your people every time they do a task well, and be detailed and specific about what they did and what made it so good in your eyes

- Recognise, acknowledge and reward people's contributions

- Facilitate access to informal and formal development opportunities, training, coaching, mentoring and work shadowing to support and encourage personal development

- Expect your people to develop at different rates and perform in different ways, and encourage them to support each other's diversity

A STRATEGIC FRAMEWORK

A COHERENT STRATEGY

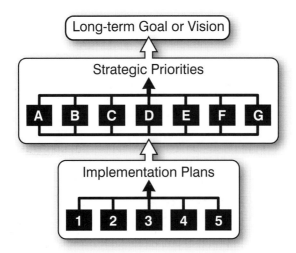

Long-term Goal or Vision

Strategic Priorities

| A | B | C | D | E | F | G |

Implementation Plans

| 1 | 2 | 3 | 4 | 5 |

A STRATEGIC FRAMEWORK

A COHERENT STRATEGY

Addressing equal opportunity effectively, and creating a culture that values difference and seeks to benefit from diversity, requires a clear vision of the future.

Once there is a vision, which should ideally be capable of being conveyed in a maximum of three sentences, then it is possible to develop an effective strategy designed to move the organisation towards the vision. With that in place you can then develop appropriate implementation plans to achieve the strategic priorities.

Most organisations - even those with many equal opportunity and/or diversity policies, programmes or projects - do not have a clear diversity vision or a strategy for bringing about change.

I believe it is vital for organisations to have a vision of the future when seeking to deliver equal opportunity and benefit from diversity.

A COHERENT STRATEGY

Many people are sceptical about the idea of 'vision' and scoff at the thought of time spent 'visioning'. Yet most of us, when thinking about a relatively mundane activity like decorating (or getting someone else to decorate) a room in our home, will have a 'vision of the future'. Answering the question, 'What will it look like when it's done?', is one of the most important things that those charged with developing effective equal opportunity and diversity policies can do.

It is not possible to develop a credible strategy without knowing what it will look like when it's done. When it comes to the diversity agenda, a number of key elements need to be included in the list of strategic priorities, no matter what the vision.

Image, leadership and accountability are vital components. Beyond that, other strategic priorities could include: communication; equal opportunity legislation; developing a culture of equality; and developing a recruitment process designed to attract more diverse job applicants.

A STRATEGIC FRAMEWORK

IMAGE, LEADERSHIP AND ACCOUNTABILITY

Every organisation I have worked with has needed to prioritise image, leadership and accountability when it comes to addressing equality issues. Addressing these issues is vital if there is to be real progress on this agenda.

How organisations are perceived by those outside, and the nature and consistency of the leadership and the extent to which the leadership is accountable and holds others to account, determines the quality of the relationships within the organisation and between the organisation and others with whom it relates.

Leaders must make it crystal clear what outcomes - in terms of quality of relationships, teamworking, individual performance, etc - they require their direct reports to achieve and what they are going to hold them accountable for. Numerical targets, relating to types of people in particular roles or grades, must only be part - and not even the most important part - of the story. Those reporting to them also need to know that there will be different consequences for them, depending on the degree of their success or failure.

A COMMUNICATION STRATEGY

Many organisations committed to equality and valuing diversity have failed to make sufficient headway because they do not have a communication strategy. Good communication is important generally, but in this context it is vital because when it comes to diversity and equality everybody believes they have something at stake. Moreover a lot of people believe they are going to lose out.

The communication strategy must ensure that:

- All staff are aware of the diversity vision and strategy, and the role they have to play in fulfilling the vision

- Relevant partners, other stakeholders and the community at large understand the organisation's commitment to:
  - Valuing and benefiting from diversity
  - Serving all customers/clients fairly and equally
  - Recruiting, developing and retaining increasingly diverse, talented, high-performing individuals

A STRATEGIC FRAMEWORK

EQUAL OPPORTUNITY LEGISLATION

At the very least, organisations need to provide information, training and/or development opportunities to ensure that all staff have a basic understanding of equal opportunity legislation and are kept up to date with changes.

Relevant staff - recruitment, other HR professionals and diversity champions - should have a more in-depth understanding of the anti-discrimination legislation and the implications for the organisation's day-to-day working practices.

A STRATEGIC FRAMEWORK

DEVELOPING A CULTURE OF EQUALITY

Developing a culture of equality, in which all staff believe that they are being treated equally well, is an obvious strategic priority for this agenda.

If people look on equal opportunity as, 'having an active expectation of access to - and a real choice to participate in or contribute to - activities or processes, believing that they are receiving relevant and appropriate treatment in relation to their ability and circumstances', then what staff **believe** about their treatment is important.

Addressing any disbelief, and turning it around, is vital if they are to contribute fully to the organisation. Organisations committed to benefiting from diversity cannot afford to be complacent about how their practice is perceived. Blaming the staff for being cynical and disbelieving simply won't do.

Attempting to bury or spin bad news, from staff surveys and the like, on the basis that it will 'disappoint the board', 'annoy top management' or 'demoralise HR and middle managers', simply stores up trouble for the future.

A STRATEGIC FRAMEWORK

DEVELOPING A PROCESS TO ATTRACT MORE DIVERSE JOB APPLICANTS

Those concerned with recruitment need to check current policies and processes to discover who are attracted to apply, which groups are missing, at what point in the recruitment process do particular groups drop out, where adverts are placed, who are featured in brochures and so on. This will identify what action, if any, is necessary to ensure that women, people with disabilities, members of minority ethnic groups and others whose talents may have been under-used in the past, are encouraged and given every opportunity to contribute to the work of the organisation.

Often, organisations find that they have to take specific action to inform members of 'traditionally marginalised groups' about their organisation and the career and job opportunities available to them, and then encourage eligible applicants to apply.

The strategic intention here is very clear, but if there is to be a successful outcome, it goes well beyond the remit of the 'recruitment team'. At the very least, the strategic priorities concerned with image and communication will also be very relevant.

A STRATEGIC FRAMEWORK

MAKING IT WORK

An effective strategy needs to be overseen by a Strategy Board led by someone at or near the top of the organisation. The Strategy Board should include the main stakeholders and should meet at least four times each year. One of its purposes is to keep the issues on everybody else's agenda. Quarterly meetings, with progress reports from all the key players, is one way of doing this.

The specific implementation plans designed to achieve the strategic priorities should be related to, and be the responsibility of, the department or functional area into which they fall - marketing, production, recruitment, etc. They should cover a period of at least twelve months and be reviewed quarterly by the Strategy Board.

If any new perceptions, policies, priorities or practices regarding diversity and equality are to be self-sustaining, and that should surely be the aim, then the strategy must ensure that they are integrated into those existing priorities and practices that are critical to the organisation's success. It is therefore vital that new ways of thinking and being, in the area of diversity and equality, become part of (and not held apart from) the culture of the organisation.

GETTING VALUE
FROM DIVERSITY

WHAT'S IN IT FOR ME?

If you are a manager or supervisor you need to get good at helping your people to see what's in it for them. You need to get very focused on the benefits that can accrue for the team and individuals when they seek value from their individual differences. If your people can see the benefits...

- Better personal relationships
- More effective teamwork
- Wider range of ideas
- More scope for problem-solving
- More enrichment of personal lives and so on

...they may be more inclined to learn how to get the benefits. You won't need to be on at them to 'keep the rules'.

IMPACT OF MANAGERS/SUPERVISORS

As a manager/supervisor you are pivotal in the matter of 'value from diversity', as in so many things in the workplace. If your team don't see you living 'it', they will pay little attention to what you say. Even if they do take notice of what you say, the chances are they will behave differently when you're not around.

It is vital therefore that as managers and supervisors you recognise what's in it for you. What's at stake is all your people feeling valued, conscious that they are making a contribution and believing their effort is acknowledged and appreciated. In short, all of your people knowing that they are included in the team. How you treat them and, more importantly, how they feel about their treatment, will determine the extent to which they feel included rather than excluded.

IMPACT OF MANAGERS/SUPERVISORS

In one course that I run hundreds of people have told me of their bad experiences where managers and supervisors have:

- Not provided guidance or support
- Not given clear goals
- Shown favouritism
- Taken credit due to their staff
- Bullied people
- Shown no interest in their people
- Ignored their ideas
- Blocked requests for learning and development programmes
- Told people they have no potential

IMPACT OF MANAGERS/SUPERVISORS

Unsurprisingly, this poor treatment affects how people feel.
They have told me that they feel:

- Unconfident
- Unhappy
- Stressed
- Like not going into work
- They want to leave
- Physically sick
- Like skiving all the time
- Excluded
- Discriminated against

- Demotivated
- They have nothing to offer
- Unappreciated

IMPACT OF MANAGERS/SUPERVISORS

Feelings affect performance. No matter how strong willed we are or how committed we are to doing the job, irrespective of distractions, how we feel will affect our productivity and the quality of our work.

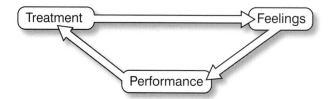

IMPACT OF MANAGERS/SUPERVISORS

How we treat others is often affected by the assumptions we make about the groups to which they belong. And how we treat others will influence how they feel. And how they are feeling will affect their performance.

Similarly, our behaviour/performance will influence how others treat us. So, manage your own inclusion by consciously and actively taking responsibility for your own feelings and consequently your behaviour/performance. And learn to control your feelings in order to influence the way you are treated.

Manage the inclusion of others more effectively by providing quality treatment, even when faced with their negative feelings and behaviours.

GETTING VALUE FROM DIVERSITY

SATISFYING DIVERSE CUSTOMERS/CLIENTS

There is huge benefit to be gained by becoming excellent at satisfying diverse customer and client groups.

Most trading organisations have for years recognised that their markets are made up of different segments. In the UK's class-conscious society, A, B, C1, C2, D and E have long been used as a way of segmenting the market economically.

There is still scope for more business benefits through segmentation, especially when it comes to minority ethnic communities. Increasing our understanding of the different cultures and sub-cultures of minority ethnic groups is critical if we are to successfully target our sales drives, for instance.

Public service providers have traditionally operated on the basis that those who need the services will find their way to them. This has now given way to thinking that recognises that there are 'hard-to-reach groups' and that providers need to take positive action to reach out to them.

SATISFYING DIVERSE CUSTOMERS/CLIENTS

The most important thing that can be done to provide a more effective service, more efficiently, to hard-to-reach groups is to engage in dialogue with them. This needs to be more than a survey and should be seen as an on-going process rather than a one off activity.

Organisations with a workforce that reflects the communities they serve, and/or the markets they sell into, are clearly in a good position to be proactive when it comes to satisfying diverse customers/clients. However, they need to demonstrate that they value the diversity of their staff if they are to be successful in engaging them in any effort to access hard-to-reach clients and customers.

NOTES

GETTING INTO ACTION

REQUIREMENTS

If an organisation is to progress in terms of diversity there needs to be personal commitment, a coherent strategy and relevant organisation activity/processes.

Someone with seniority and influence in the organisation must be committed to recognising and getting value from diversity. Unless there is at least one person with a strong commitment, the chances are there will be little or no progress, and any progress that is made will be difficult to sustain.

There must be a coherent strategy with clearly defined implementation plans, which when accomplished will move the organisation towards the long-term goal.

The five D's - desire, definition, decision, determination and **discipline** - can help organisations to get into action and stay on track.

DESIRE

Does the organisation, or at least the part of the organisation that makes and drives the policy priorities, have a desire to address the issue? Is there a pull towards the benefits of diversity and an understanding of the importance of managing inclusion? Or is it simply a push away from the fear of being caught discriminating against certain groups or individuals?

How strong is your desire?	Yes	No
Do you believe that more diversity means more potential?		
Do you want to see more gender balance in senior management?		
Do you expect your people to do things differently to the same standard?		
Is it necessary to offer training and support to staff who want to leave?		
Would you like to see a more diverse customer base?		
Is it necessary to actively target hard-to-reach customers/clients?		

The more 'yes' answers you give, the stronger your desire.

DEFINITION

Many organisations become active around the diversity agenda without ever properly defining what they mean and being clear about what it is they want to achieve. The clearer you can be about your goal, the better the chance of staying on track. This is true no matter what the area of work and it is vital when it comes to seeking value from diversity.

So, describe the vision: what will it look like when it's done?

_____

_____

_____

_____

_____

DECISION

It is important that a decision is taken to actively seek to realise the vision rather than, as is often the case, simply to agree that diversity is rather a good idea. The relevant body needs to decide that action will be taken to move towards the vision. They need also to decide who will be responsible for ensuring the goals are achieved and who they are accountable to for achieving them.

DETERMINATION

Organisations setting out to achieve value from diversity need to see it as a long-term process. This is not to say there will not be 'quick wins' and benefits that show up in the short-term - benefits such as improved personal relationships, better communication and improved attendances and timekeeping. However, for productivity gains, accessing new markets or hard-to-reach client groups and increasing the diversity of the management team, you need to take a longer-term view.

The team driving the process will be subject to criticism - more or less sustained, and from two opposite poles.

DETERMINATION

Firstly, you will be criticised for not moving quickly enough. Your 'slow pace' will be proof of your lack of commitment. You need to stay consistent at this stage:

1. Restate 'what it will look like when it's done'.
2. Demonstrate that you are on track in relation to the implementation plans if, indeed, you are.
3. Explain why there is slippage against the plans, if there is, and what action will be taken and when to get back on track.
4. Whether on track or not, tell the criticisers that you would value their help, and ask them how they will contribute to achieving the implementation plan and/or how they think the plan could be improved.

Secondly, you will be criticised for 'going over the top', 'positive discrimination', 'wasting resources', 'being politically correct' and so on. You should ask this group to consider whether it makes sense to try and get the maximum productive effort for a fair wage from all employees and not just those like themselves. They will no doubt say, 'yes'. This will set you up to explain what the organisation is trying to achieve through the diversity work. It's best to stay focused on the business benefits and what you are expecting to get from those they perceive you to be discriminating in favour of.

DISCIPLINE

A disciplined approach is called for if progress is to be made and sustained. The area where indiscipline sets in soonest is the review meeting. The regular (monthly) meeting to review progress, acknowledge achievements and reset short-term goals as necessary, is vital to maintain momentum. Yet, it is often the first casualty of an undisciplined approach.

Staying in communication with the different groups - those inside and outside the organisation who were involved in any research or planning when the diversity strategy was being formulated - is important but requires discipline. It is easy for this apparently peripheral activity to be overlooked because you are too busy 'doing the work' to talk to others about it. The communication plan should be seen as part and parcel of the work and have the same status as other areas of activity.

KEY ROLE ESSENTIAL

There has to be someone with seniority and influence who takes responsibility for ensuring that something happens. If there isn't, then things grind to halt, if indeed they ever get started. The person who has responsibility needs also to have it as a priority.

These things do not always go together when the diversity agenda is being addressed, but success is more likely if they can be brought together.

FOCUS ON WHAT YOU WANT

With diversity and equality there is a strong tendency for organisations to focus most, if not all, of their energy on what they want to avoid or stamp out rather than what they want to achieve. This leads to policies and programmes being created around avoiding unlawful and unnecessary discrimination, dealing with harassment and ensuring that nobody receives unfair treatment.

It is right and proper to want to avoid these things, but the best way to do that is to stay focused on what you want - active inclusion, value from diversity, quality treatment for all, etc. However you articulate it, the key is to accentuate the positive things you want rather than dwell on the negative things you are trying to avoid.

GETTING INTO ACTION

BE PREPARED TO DO THINGS DIFFERENTLY

One thing is certain, if you are to achieve your diversity aspirations: you will have to do things differently. It stands to reason that if you haven't got what you want from what you have been doing, then you need to do things differently or, heaven forbid, do different things. It is surprising how relatively easy it is to set objectives and decide that things need to be different, and then discover that nobody can find anything that they think needs to be changed or done differently.

Sometimes the very people you are trying to 'include' - clients/customers from hard-to-reach groups and employees who are members of traditionally marginalised groups - are unsure what could be done differently, even when asked directly. You need to consistently assure them of your preparedness to do things differently, and actively encourage them to come back to you every time they discover something that they think could be done differently to achieve the diversity goals.

MAKE SURE THE MUSIC FITS THE WORDS

Congruence is the key here. There needs to be consistency between the organisation's policies and priorities and its practice. Every time anyone fails to practise what the organisation preaches there will be dissonance and discord, and those concerned with that particular part of the organisation's performance will 'hear' that the music does not fit the words.

Senior managers and executives in particular need to ensure that they 'walk the talk' because they will come in for close scrutiny on this agenda. How they behave in their private offices and how they treat junior staff and those who report to them will be common knowledge, no matter how 'private' they thought it was.

Walking the talk, or not, will be an important litmus test of whether the organisation is succeeding or failing to achieve its diversity objectives.

APPRAISALS: INCLUDE DIVERSITY

Ensure that diversity objectives are taken into account in annual appraisals. Of course, to do this you must first make sure everyone has diversity objectives (see page 104). The objectives need to be relevant to the particular work role and must be recognised and acknowledged as such by the appraiser. Whether the objective is achieved or not achieved must be noted and be clearly seen to make a difference to the marking and/or commentary and/or learning and development plan that follows the appraisal.

GETTING INTO ACTION

RECOGNISE <u>YOU</u> HAVE TO DO SOMETHING

Whoever you are and wherever you fit in the organisation, you have to do something if you want things on the diversity agenda to be different. You cannot be a passenger and simply hope that someone else will do something. You have to be that 'someone' if you want things to change. The very least you can do is to get this book into the hands of whoever you think has the authority and/or the commitment and/or the influence to make things happen.

Whatever you do, don't just read about it - **TAKE SOME ACTION.**

RETAINING/RECRUITING A MORE DIVERSE WORKFORCE

RETAINING/RECRUITING A MORE DIVERSE WORKFORCE

THE FIVE C's

In this section we are going to consider five C's - commitment, challenge, culture, contribution and community.

COMMITMENT
It is vital that the organisation is committed to having a more diverse workforce. If there is no real commitment, then the policies and day-to-day priorities of the organisation will not reflect, or even take account of, the diversity objectives. Commitment needs to be seen from the top of the organisation (though it doesn't necessarily have to start there).

CHALLENGE

Many organisations face enormous challenges in attracting a more diverse workforce because how they look, or are perceived, will dictate who applies to join. So, no matter what the current employee make-up, if you want it to be more diverse than it is already, you will need to be vigorously proactive.

To reach the 'missing groups' you will need to engage in **outreach activities**. They won't just find their way to you simply because you advertise your vacancies in the appropriate paper. There are five interrelated steps to take in order to attract individuals from the 'missing groups':

1. Assess the present situation
2. Decide the specific aims of the outreach programme
3. Find out as much as you can about the target group
4. Develop and implement an action plan
5. Review progress and revise plan as necessary

Many organisations want to have a more ethnically diverse workforce, so I will take minority ethnic communities as my example, as I work through the five steps on the following pages.

RETAINING/RECRUITING A MORE DIVERSE WORKFORCE

CHALLENGE

STEP 1: ASSESS THE PRESENT SITUATION

Gather necessary background information:

- Which minority ethnic communities are present in your travel to work area?
- What proportion of the overall population do they represent?
- What proportion of current employees is of minority ethnic origin?
- How does this compare with the proportion of those economically active in the minority ethnic communities?
- What proportion of minority ethnic employees are in each grade/role?
- What proportion of recent applicants was of minority ethnic origin?
- What proportion of recent appointees was of minority ethnic origin?
- What proportion of recent leavers was of minority ethnic origin?

CHALLENGE

STEP 1: ASSESS THE PRESENT SITUATION

Identify areas of concern/under-representation:

Analysing the data gathered in answer to the questions in the previous section will
enable you to identify those areas requiring attention. These might include:

- Minority ethnic 'under-representation' generally
- Minority ethnic 'under-representation' in particular grades/roles
- Low level of minority ethnic applicants
- Lower success rate of minority ethnic applicants

CHALLENGE

STEP 2: DECIDE SPECIFIC AIMS

The overall aims for the outreach programme will obviously need to take account of any wider organisation aims or objectives, and will clearly need to reflect the business needs and local conditions. For example:

- Ensuring that the relevant minority ethnic communities understand the organisation's commitment to creating a more diverse workforce

- Ensuring that influential members of the relevant minority ethnic communities are aware of the organisation and the career opportunities on offer

- Building long-term links with those organisations and institutions capable of informing or influencing potential minority ethnic applicants

- Ensuring that suitably qualified potential applicants of minority ethnic origin are aware of specific vacancies as and when they occur

RETAINING/RECRUITING A MORE DIVERSE WORKFORCE

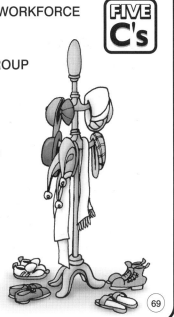

FIVE C's

CHALLENGE

STEP 3: FIND OUT ABOUT THE TARGET GROUP

- Consult the 2001 census data
- Talk to the Commission for Equality and Human Rights and/or the local Equality and Human Rights Council
- Talk to anyone you know who belongs to or has links with the target group: your organisation may already employ a small number of such employees
- Approach places of worship and community centres

The more you know, and are seen to know, about the target group, in terms of cultures, priorities, preferences etc, the more accurately you will be able to target your promotional work. You will also be demonstrating your commitment to involve them in the organisation by the very act of researching the relevant group.

CHALLENGE

STEP 4: THE ACTION PLAN

Clearly, the shape and content of the plan will depend on the outcome of steps 1, 2 and 3 and the resources allocated. However, your approach might include all or a combination of the following:

Building links with minority ethnic communities generally:

- Develop relationships with the leadership of key organisations
- Ask for their help – make specific requests
- Invite representatives of key organisations to visit your organisation
- Provide speakers for meetings of relevant community organisations
- Organise open days and social events
- Produce information in the relevant 'mother tongue'
- Use the minority ethnic media - send them your press releases

CHALLENGE

STEP 4: THE ACTION PLAN

Building links with young people of minority ethnic origin:

- Develop relationships with schools, colleges, careers advisors etc, to make them aware of your ambitions
- Offer work experience and work shadowing
- Develop relationships with youth clubs
- Sponsor a relevant local sports team or league

Informing minority ethnic communities of specific vacancies:

- Send information about vacancies to the key organisations
- Develop a database of influential individuals and keep them regularly informed
- Communicate directly with existing minority ethnic employees
- Use specialist recruitment agencies when large numbers of vacancies occur
- Advertise in the minority ethnic media

CHALLENGE

STEP 5: REVIEW PROGRESS

Review progress on a regular basis so that actions can be adjusted in the light of experience. Reviewing on a quarterly basis is recommended.

- Assess outcomes against the original objectives
- Identify any unplanned and/or unexpected consequences and impact
- Talk to those who had been consulted in steps 1 to 4
- Revise actions as necessary

CHALLENGE

Organisation profile is important when considering an outreach programme, and it is a key element in its own right. The following questions might be worth considering:

- Does the organisation have a profile in the target community?

- If 'yes', how is it perceived?

- If their perception is not our reality, what action will we take?

Alligators in the lobby

If they think you've got alligators in the lobby people won't cross it, not even to get an application form for the job of their dreams. Actively address their perceptions, don't wait for them to somehow discover that the alligators are not real.

(73)

RETAINING/RECRUITING A MORE DIVERSE WORKFORCE

CULTURE

The culture of the organisation is a key issue with regard to retention of people who are, by definition, different from the majority or from those who are in positions of control or influence. I define culture simply as, **'the way we do things around here'**. There are numerous books written on the culture of organisations, so I will not labour the point. I will, however, offer three more C's to help focus on some important elements in the context of diversity.

1. Clarity
2. Congruence (again)
3. Consistency

Clarity is important for everyone in a workplace, but it is vital for those who might not yet be part of the 'mainstream'. Ideally, the culture should be one that facilitates clarity about the standards required, clarity about when things need to be finished/delivered and clarity about methods of communication and protocol generally. Clarity means ensuring that the 'ground rules' are explicit and not simply assumed.

RETAINING/RECRUITING A MORE DIVERSE WORKFORCE

CULTURE

Congruence is about managers and supervisors 'walking the talk.' Do those with power and influence live up to the stated policies and priorities when it comes to valuing diversity? Is there congruence between what they say and what they do and between their public and private behaviours? Do their direct reports feel that their differences are valued?

Consistency can be a decisive factor for a newcomer trying to determine whether an organisation is going to value them? Does the sense of being wanted last beyond the first month? Does the good quality treatment extend beyond their immediate work team? Whether people stay or go will be determined by how valued they feel. The culture, 'the way we do things around here', will speak far more loudly than the stated policies, rules and regulations. So, the extent to which your organisation culture is one that consistently seeks value from diversity will be vital.

COMMUNITY

Creating a sense of community (of belonging) within the organisation is an important way of keeping staff turnover down. People will be encouraged to stay because of this rather than because they have nowhere else to go. Actively facilitating access is the key to developing and maintaining a good sense of community. All employees need access to:

- Relevant information
- Support networks
- Learning and development programmes
- Reward processes
- Advancement and promotion opportunities

CONTRIBUTION

Most of us want to feel that we contribute to society generally. We also want to contribute in our place of employment. We feel good when our contributions make a difference and add value to the whole. I believe this is a normal human emotion. As a key part of a retention strategy, organisations need to actively seek contributions by:

- Identifying and utilizing experience, knowledge and skills unique to individual employees
- Involving all employees in discussing and developing new ideas, processes and products
- Encouraging managers/supervisors to seek feedback from their team members
- Encouraging employees to discuss new ideas and approaches in team meetings
- Praising people when they deserve it

NOTES

CHAMPIONING DIVERSITY

CHAMPIONING DIVERSITY

THE DIVERSITY CHAMPION

It is useful, possibly vital, to have a designated diversity champion or two in the organisation. They need to have influence and authority, and recognise the need for and be prepared to continue their own diversity education. They should ideally be appointed by the Board and be seen to be taking the role seriously. They should have a Diversity & Inclusion Coach to support them in their difficult task, because if anyone in the organisation needs to be seen to be 'walking the talk', the champions do!

The role of the champion is to:

1. Inform and educate their peers about the organisation's diversity vision and strategy - how it is relevant to and connected with the organisation's purpose and functions
2. Support directors/executives with the diversity aspects of their business plans
3. Facilitate access to information, people and networks, for the diversity and equality staff support groups
4. Evaluate (others should be monitoring) the impact and outcomes of the various diversity initiatives
5. Provide regular and direct feedback to the Board

INFORM AND EDUCATE

Champions must inform and educate their peers about the organisation's diversity vision and strategy - how it is relevant to and connected with the organisation's purpose and functions. The fact that addressing the diversity and equality agenda has a direct relevance to the business won't necessarily be obvious, even to very senior staff.

Champions will need to consistently go back to basics with their colleagues to help them see the business benefits of diversity and the opportunity costs of burying their heads.

Informing and educating are best done in response to comments or questions raised informally and 'off the cuff' as it were. Champions should also take opportunities to point out the relevance of diversity during discussions about 'mainstream' issues.

Addressing the questions and responding to opportunities in a direct, informative and supportive way - outside of any formal presentations or training - is a powerful way of bringing people on, without them feeling they have been put upon.

CHAMPIONING DIVERSITY

SUPPORT DIRECTORS

Directors and senior executives will need help in building diversity into their business plan, and champions must be able to offer guidance and support.

Inviting them to address three questions about the implications of diversity may be a useful way of triggering their thinking (even if the champion knows little about the specific area of work):

1. Are there groups of potential customers/clients that we are failing to reach and, if so, how much do we know about them?

2. Do we have any employees who are from those groups?
   a) If so, how involved are they in any efforts to reach them?
   b) If not, should we be seeking to target them for employment?

3. How could we better utilize the unique experience, knowledge and skills of **all** the existing staff?

CHAMPIONING DIVERSITY

FACILITATE ACCESS

Networks and staff support groups are often established (or simply form themselves) around different diversity and equality issues. An important part of the champion's role is to help these groups to tap into the organisation's 'mainframe' so that they can quickly access relevant information. This will enable them to bring their particular perspective to bear on policy ideas as they are being developed.

It's also useful for the leadership of the organisation to be able to sit down from time to time with representatives of the 'women in management network' or the 'gay and lesbian concerns group' or the 'minority ethnic support group' or the 'disabilities concern group' etc. Far better to have on-going, easy access rather than just the set-piece dialogue when a new policy is about to be launched or when there is an issue. The champion should be oiling wheels and brokering relationships between the relevant parties.

Facilitating access is often unseen and behind the scenes but it is vital work that requires the champion to build and maintain trust. Champions sometimes have to take risks to head off conflicts that they can foresee because of their access to the thinking and priorities of the inner circle of the organisation. Those who are unprepared to take those risks often lose credibility with the networks/staff support groups because they fail to alert them to relevant changes.

CHAMPIONING DIVERSITY

EVALUATE OUTCOMES

The diversity champion or champions should be concerned about impact and outcomes. At each review of the strategy or implementation plan they should ask themselves three simple questions:

1. To what extent have the tasks described in the implementation plans been completed?
2. Have the completed tasks achieved the strategic priorities?
3. Are the strategic priorities still the appropriate way to move towards the diversity vision in the light of changed circumstances?

In the early days, it is likely that the monitoring process will not be sufficiently advanced to enable the champion to get satisfactory answers to the questions. If this happens, then in order to help the organization stay on track, the task is to put processes in place that will enable the above three questions to be answered.

PROVIDE REGULAR FEEDBACK

The champion must keep the Board and/or senior management team up to speed about what's going on with the diversity agenda, whether they want to know or not! Champions should not wait to be asked, but should make sure that they report back on a formal basis at least twice a year and ideally quarterly.

Champions should also take opportunities to identify and highlight the connections between the 'business' agenda and the diversity vision and strategy.

The Board's thinking about the diversity agenda should be regularly fed back to the Diversity Strategy Board who should be in no doubt as to the level of commitment and concerns of the Board. Champions should not be 'sugaring the pill', either to make the Board appear more committed than it is, or to make the Board think more progress is being made than is the case.

(85)

CHAMPIONING DIVERSITY

WITHIN YOUR TEAM/DEPARTMENT

USEFUL TIPS

- Specifically acknowledge every member of your team in a 'personal meeting' - however short - every month
- During the 'meeting' let them know that you believe they have the capacity to learn, grow and develop, and be a high quality performer
- Find out about the knowledge, skills and interests of your staff and encourage them to share them with other colleagues
- Be aware how diverse your team is, and might look to others, and actively seek benefit from the differences
- Be an active listener to all your team members, especially those who might appear not to be listened to by other colleagues
- Be a considerate communicator - check that what you've asked someone to do has been understood in line with your expectations
- Invite (and expect) feedback, and demonstrate behavioural change in response to it
- Praise your people publicly and give them constructive criticism in private (if criticism is not intended to be constructive, then consider not giving it at all)
- Coach, support and encourage your staff to do all the above, and recognise and reward them for it

DEALING WITH ISSUES

DEMONSTRATE COMMITMENT

When diversity and equality issues and concerns arise it is important that all people, but especially those with the grievance, are able to recognise and acknowledge the organisation's commitment to working to achieve the diversity vision. An audit trail of Board decisions, resources committed, progress reports of actions taken, and so on could be helpful here. It would be far more helpful though if the management were perceived to be 'walking the talk'.

In hearing a complaint two things are important:

- Firstly, demonstrate that you are prepared to listen - deliberately divert the phone, turn off the sound of the computer, come out from behind the desk, etc

- Secondly, make it clear that you take the complaint or concern seriously and that you will deal with it as a matter of urgency

CONSIDER OPTIONS

Many issues of concern will not contravene any anti-discrimination legislation. They may not even be against the organisation's rules/policies. However, they will, by definition, be perceived as excluding. And if they are perceived that way, then they are - even if that wasn't the intention.

It will be important therefore to engage the complainant in a conversation about options. When diversity and equality issues arise, the possible range of actions that could be taken is vast. Talking through the possible actions and their probable consequences – while encouraging the complainant to share their ideas – is an important conversation to have in order to ensure that the complainant is not surprised by the eventual recommendation you make.

Close the conversation by informing the complainant that you intend to reflect on the different options discussed (listing each one), consult with relevant colleagues and will get back to them on (named) day. Depending on the organisation culture, this should be no more than three working days, otherwise your commitment to treating it as a matter of urgency could look pretty shabby.

DEALING WITH ISSUES

COMMUNICATE AND TAKE ACTION

On or before the agreed date, meet with the 'complainant' to share your recommendation. Make sure you provide time for a discussion and not just an 'announcement'.

Ideally, the approach you recommend will have been one of the options discussed and will provide space for the complainant to influence your thinking and subsequent actions.

At the end of the meeting ensure that the complainant fully understands your recommended approach and is clear about what you judge the probable outcomes/implications could be. Immediately after the meeting, send an e-mail or memo confirming your joint understanding.

(90) **Take action and do what you said you would do!**

THE DIVERSITY CHECKLIST

THE DIVERSITY CHECKLIST

STAYING FOCUSED

Staying focused on the diversity agenda means:

- Valuing diversity from the top
- Articulating the vision
- Awareness education
- Enlisting support at all levels
- Developing diversity in decision-making groups
- Reflecting diversity in payment policies
- Encouraging networks and support groups
- Effective equal opportunity policies
- Monitoring and evaluation

THE DIVERSITY CHECKLIST

VALUING DIVERSITY FROM THE TOP

To what extent does the most senior body in the organisation take responsibility for the diversity vision?

How does the leadership demonstrate that the organisation is open and accessible, keen to reflect the diversity of the markets/communities it serves, and striving to utilize all available talent?

How does the 'boss' hold all direct reports to account for setting and achieving personal diversity objectives?

To what extent does the strategic/business planning process include the diversity vision and priorities?

THE DIVERSITY CHECKLIST

ARTICULATING THE VISION

ITEM 1 ☑
ITEM 2 ☐
ITEM 3 ☐
ITEM 4 ☐
ITEM 5 ☐

How and where are Board members and other senior staff articulating the diversity vision?

How is the diversity vision reflected in the organisation's business objectives and priorities?

How effective is the communication plan in ensuring that all staff are aware of the diversity vision and strategy and the fact that they have a role to play in the vision being fulfilled?

THE DIVERSITY CHECKLIST

AWARENESS EDUCATION

How much access do staff have to information and/or programmes to keep them up to date with equality legislation?

How effective are the specific learning and development programmes/processes designed to inform and educate staff about the issues associated with diversity and inclusion?

To what extent do all learning and development programmes reflect the organisation's diversity and equality aspirations?

THE DIVERSITY CHECKLIST

ENLISTING SUPPORT AT ALL LEVELS

On a scale of 1 to 10 (10 is high) how committed are all employees to the diversity vision, and what will be done to increase their buy-in?

Board/executive level

Senior managers

Middle managers/specialists

First-line managers/supervisors

Production/front-line staff

THE DIVERSITY CHECKLIST

DEVELOPING DIVERSITY IN DECISION-MAKING GROUPS

Most organisations operate on the basis that decision-making and hierarchy are inextricably linked even when the decision is taken by, or involves, a group rather than an individual.

This need not be the case, especially when an organisation is conscious that particular groups are 'under-represented' at senior levels. Deciding to uncouple the decision-making process from the system of accountability could be extremely liberating for organisations.

Creating decision-making groups that reflect the diversity of background, experience, skills and talents of employees would probably radically increase the innovative potential of most organisations. The accountability process would remain the same and the hierarchy would still have to 'carry the can' and be held responsible for the good governance of the organisation.

In which areas of your work could you increase the diversity of the decision-making group?

REFLECTING DIVERSITY GOALS IN PAYMENT POLICIES

How could the organisation better reflect commitment to the diversity vision through its payment policies?

THE DIVERSITY CHECKLIST

ENCOURAGING NETWORKS AND SUPPORT GROUPS

How do we facilitate, encourage and involve support groups and employee networks?

How could we increase their understanding of our wider diversity vision and strategy?

How could we increase their appreciation of the role and importance of the other networks?

How could we involve them more closely in developing our strategy and creating implementation plans to move us towards our diversity vision?

THE DIVERSITY CHECKLIST

EFFECTIVE EQUAL OPPORTUNITY POLICIES

On what basis do we measure the effectiveness of our equal opportunity policies?

_____

_____

To what extent do the policies affect the day-to-day working practices of the organisation?

_____

_____

How do we ensure that the policies are kept up-to-date with changes in legislation?

_____

_____

THE DIVERSITY CHECKLIST

MONITORING AND EVALUATION

To what extent do we have a framework for collecting, analysing and utilizing data regarding diversity issues relevant to the organisation?

How frequently do we review existing data collecting processes and determine what else needs to be done?

How do we evaluate the effectiveness of the diversity strategy?

NOTES

SETTING PERSONAL DIVERSITY & INCLUSION OBJECTIVES

SETTING PERSONAL DIVERSITY & INCLUSION OBJECTIVES

FOCUSED SELF-QUESTIONING

One way of identifying relevant goals and setting meaningful personal objectives in the area of diversity and inclusion is to engage in a process of focused self-questioning. The following questions are designed to enable you to identify clear and specific personal objectives, to enable you to take your organisation's diversity and equality work further.

Health warning: You may find this difficult and/or embarrassing!

SETTING PERSONAL DIVERSITY & INCLUSION OBJECTIVES

FOCUSED SELF-QUESTIONING

1. What do I know about the diversity and inclusion ambitions of my organisation?
    (This is not simply about numerical recruitment, retention or promotion targets.)

_____

_____

_____

2. In what ways does my approach to my main work priorities move my organisation
    towards its diversity and inclusion ambitions?

_____

_____

_____

FOCUSED SELF-QUESTIONING

3. How in-tune is my thinking about diversity and inclusion with my organisation's diversity and equality policy/priorities?

_____

_____

_____

4. How in-tune is my thinking about diversity and inclusion with the thinking of those with whom I work closely?

_____

_____

_____

FOCUSED SELF-QUESTIONING

5. In the context of diversity and inclusion, in what areas, if any, do I need to increase or improve my information, knowledge or skills?

_____

_____

_____

Given my answers to the five questions above:

6. What general areas or issues could I be addressing in order to improve my organisation's chances of getting maximum value from the diversity of the staff and/or improving the quality of the service and support it provides to customers, clients and stakeholders?

_____

_____

_____

FOCUSED SELF-QUESTIONING

7. What **specific** objectives **could** I set in order to make progress in any of the areas identified in question 6?

_____

_____

_____

8. Given my answer to question 7, what **will** my objectives be for the coming 12 months?

_____

_____

_____

FOCUSED SELF-QUESTIONING

9.   What one thing will I do tomorrow to move towards achieving my objectives?

_____

_____

_____

RESOURCES

Equality Commission for Northern Ireland
Equality House, 7-9 Shaftsbury Square, Belfast, BT2 7DP

Equality and Human Rights Commission
3 More London, Riverside, Tooley Street, SE1 2RG.
Tel: 020 3117 0235 Fax: 01925 884 275
info@equalityhumanrights.com www.equalityhumanrights.com

FURTHER READING

From Diversity to Unity
by Mary E. Casey and Geraldine M. Bown, published by iUniverse.com

Managing the Workforce 2000
by David Jamieson and Julie Omara, published by Jossey-Bass

The Diversity Training Handbook
by Phil Clements and John Jones, published by Kogan Page

Cross-cultural Business Pocketbook
by John Mattock, published by Management Pocketbooks

Developing People Pocketbook
by Ian Fleming, published by Management Pocketbooks

About the Author

Linbert Spencer

Linbert Spencer is an international consultant, trainer and coach specialising in diversity and equality, leadership, performance management and personal effectiveness. A leading authority on diversity and inclusion, he held a number of key public and voluntary sector appointments before setting up his own consultancy business in 1990.

His clients include multinational manufacturing and service corporations, major government departments – including the Foreign Office, as well as various police organisations.

Linbert is a keynote speaker, has coached many top executives and senior civil servants, regularly facilitates learning events at board and senior executive level and has designed several personal effectiveness and career development programmes. His consultancy is a UK National Training Award winner and facilitates learning and development programmes all over the world for global organisations.

Linbert co-founded the Windsor Fellowship, a national charity that prepares minority ethnic undergraduates for management roles. He serves on various bodies including the Foreign Office Diversity Strategy Board, the MOD's Defence Business Learning Advisory Board, the Churches Commission for Racial Justice, and the Boards of Youth at Risk and the Salvation Army Housing Association.

Contact
Linbert Spencer Consultancy, 3 Abbey Square, Turvey, Bedfordshire, MK43 8DJ
E-mail: linbertspencer@hotmail.com Website: www.linbertspencer.com

ORDER FORM

Your details

Name _____

Position _____

Company _____

Address _____

_____

_____

Telephone _____

Fax _____

E-mail _____

VAT No. (EC companies) _____

Your Order Ref _____

Please send me:

	No. copies
The Diversity _____ Pocketbook	[ ]
The _____ Pocketbook	[ ]
The _____ Pocketbook	[ ]
The _____ Pocketbook	[ ]

Order by Post

MANAGEMENT POCKETBOOKS LTD

LAUREL HOUSE, STATION APPROACH, ALRESFORD, HAMPSHIRE SO24 9JH UK

Order by Phone, Fax or Internet
Telephone: +44 (0)1962 735573
Facsimile: +44 (0)1962 733637
E-mail: sales@pocketbook.co.uk
Web: www.pocketbook.co.uk

Customers in USA should contact:
Management Pocketbooks
2427 Bond Street, University Park, IL 60466
Telephone: 866 620 6944 Facsimile: 708 534 7803
E-mail: mp.orders@ware-pak.com
Web: www.managementpocketbooks.com